14/11 (6/06) 4
14/12 (11/09) 13

Bees

A DENVER MUSEUM OF NATURE & SCIENCE BOOK

 Written by **Deborah Hodge**
Illustrated by **Julian Mulock**

KIDS CAN PRESS

For Helen Hodge and Darren Bowell, with thanks for the fun!

Acknowledgments
I would like to gratefully acknowledge the invaluable comments and review of this
manuscript by Paula E. Cushing, Ph.D. curator of entomology and arachnology, Zoology Department,
Denver Museum of Nature & Science. I would also like to thank Heidi Lumberg, former publications director,
and her staff at the Denver Museum of Nature & Science Press for their helpful collaboration in this book.
Finally, a special thanks to my editor, Valerie Wyatt, who never gives up when the going gets tough.

Text © 2004 Deborah Hodge
Illustrations © 2004 Julian Mulock
Activity photographs © 2004 Ray Boudreau

Bees was produced in cooperation with the Denver Museum of Nature & Science
www.dmns.org.

Kids Can Press acknowledges the financial support of the Government of Ontario, through the
Ontario Media Development Corporation's Ontario Book Initiative; the Ontario Arts Council; the Canada
Council for the Arts; and the Government of Canada, through the BPIDP, for our publishing activity.
This book is supported in part by the Lloyd David and Carlye Cannon Wattis Foundation.

Published in Canada by   Published in the U.S. by
Kids Can Press Ltd.   Kids Can Press Ltd.
29 Birch Avenue   2250 Military Road
Toronto, ON M4V 1E2   Tonawanda, NY 14150

www.kidscanpress.com

Edited by Valerie Wyatt
Designed by Julia Naimska
Printed in Hong Kong, China, by Sheck Wah Tong Printing Press Limited

This book is smyth sewn casebound.

CM 04 0 9 8 7 6 5 4 3 2 1

National Library of Canada Cataloguing in Publication Data

Hodge, Deborah
Bees / written by Deborah Hodge ; illustrated by Julian Mulock.

(A Denver Museum of Nature & Science book.)
Includes index.
ISBN 1-55337-065-1 (bound).   ISBN 1-55337-656-0 (pbk.)

1. Bees — Juvenile literature. I. Mulock, Julian II. Denver Museum of Nature & Science III. Title.
IV. Series: Denver Museum of Nature & Science book.

QL565.2.H63 2004   j595.79'9   C2002-905568-7

Kids Can Press is a **LOTUS**™ Entertainment company

Contents

The Buzz on Bees

What has stripes and buzzes and makes honey?
A honeybee!

Ouch! Have you ever been stung by a bee? Bees sting to scare away enemies. After a honeybee stings, it dies.

A bee's buzz is the sound of its wings flapping — up to 200 times a second.

This honeybee is sipping
nectar from a flower.
Nectar is a sweet juice
that bees turn into honey.

A Honeybee

Two **antennae** help the bee touch, taste and smell.

Big eyes are made up of many tiny parts. These **compound eyes** see all around.

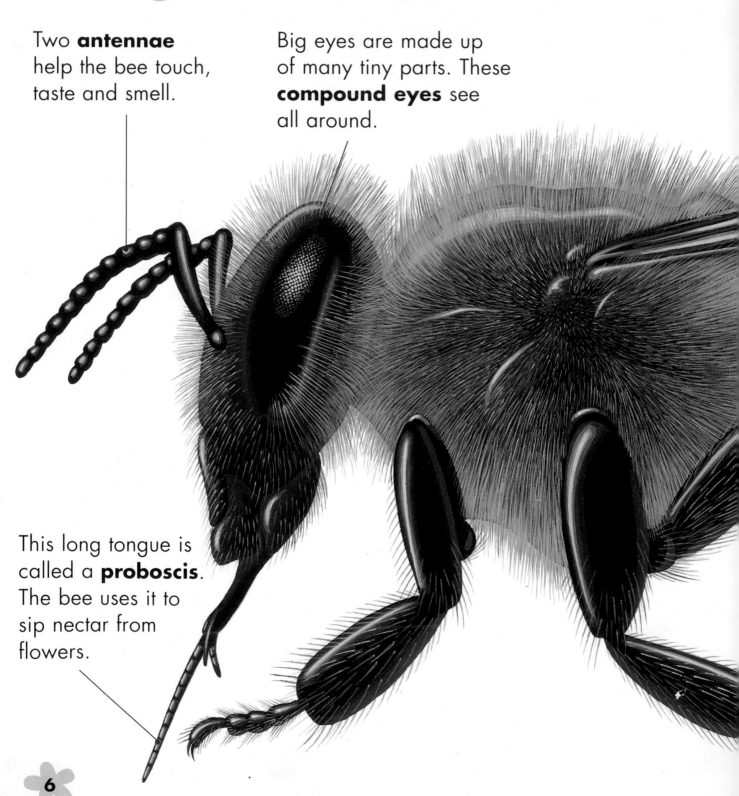

This long tongue is called a **proboscis**. The bee uses it to sip nectar from flowers.

6

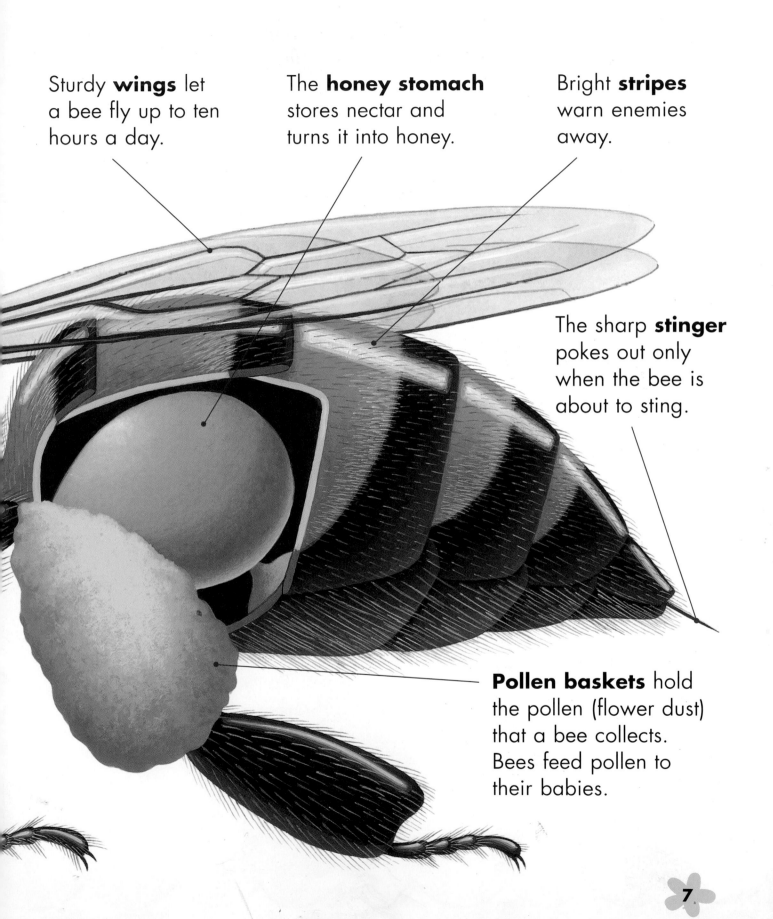

Sturdy **wings** let a bee fly up to ten hours a day.

The **honey stomach** stores nectar and turns it into honey.

Bright **stripes** warn enemies away.

The sharp **stinger** pokes out only when the bee is about to sting.

Pollen baskets hold the pollen (flower dust) that a bee collects. Bees feed pollen to their babies.

Build a Bee

Ask an adult to help you make your own bee.

What you need

- 3 Styrofoam balls — $\frac{1}{2}$ of a small round ball, 1 larger round ball, 1 egg-shaped ball
- yellow and black poster paint
- a paintbrush
- 2 toothpicks
- 6 black pipe cleaners
- scissors
- wax paper
- a brad (brass fastener)

What you do

1 Paint the balls yellow. Let them dry.

2 Join the balls with toothpicks.

3 Make stripes by wrapping pipe cleaners around the egg-shaped ball.

4 Push in 6 legs, each made from $\frac{1}{3}$ of a pipe cleaner. Push in smaller pieces of pipe cleaner for the antennae, tongue and stinger.

5 Cut wings from wax paper. Fasten them to the bee's middle section with a brad.

What's happening?
A bee is an insect. All insects have six legs and three main body parts: head, thorax and abdomen.

Head   Thorax   Abdomen

Paint on black eyes and add some glitter, if you wish.

9

Home Sweet Hive

Honeybees live everywhere in the world, except for very cold places. They live in big groups called colonies.

A colony of bees works together and shares food. The colony lives in a home called a hive.

Many honeybees live in hives built by people. This hive is cut open so you can see inside.

Up to 50 000 bees live in one hive.

These wild honeybees make their hive inside a tree. When the hive gets too crowded, some of the bees fly away in a big group to start a new hive. This is called swarming.

Busy Bees

Have you heard the saying "as busy as a bee"? Bees are very hard workers.

Some bees gather food. Others feed the baby bees. Still others guard or clean the hive or build tiny wax rooms called cells.

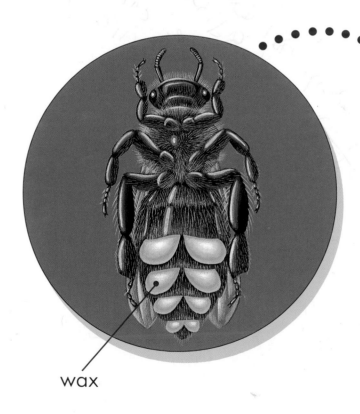

wax

This is the underside of a bee. The wax for building cells comes from its abdomen.

Peek inside a hive. These bees are building honeycomb — rows of wax cells. The cells will hold honey, pollen or baby bees.

A cell has six sides and is very strong.

13

Honeycomb Prints

Why do bees make cells with six sides?
Find out by making a honeycomb design.
Ask an adult to help you.

What you need
- paper for tracing
- scissors
- a large potato
- a paring knife
- poster paint
- light-color paper

What you do

1 Trace the six-sided shape below. Cut out the tracing.

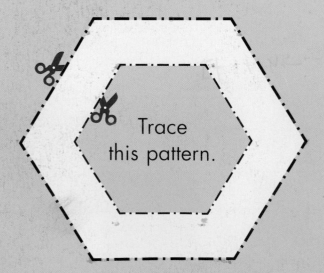

Trace this pattern.

2 Cut a thick slice of potato. Use the tracing as a guide to cut a six-sided edge on the outside and inside of the potato slice. This is your stamp.

3 Dip the stamp into the paint and press it down on the paper to make a print. Make another print beside the first one. Try to fit the prints as closely together as possible. Fill your paper with prints.

What's happening?
A shape with six equal sides is called a hexagon. The hexagon shape works well in a hive because the cells fit tightly together. There is little wasted space. Also, a hexagon is a strong shape. It lets the cells hold lots of honey.

No wasted space

Meet the Bees

Three kinds of bees live in a colony: workers, drones and a queen.

A **worker** is a female bee. Workers do the day-to-day work of the hive. Most bees in the colony are workers. They live only about four weeks.

The **queen** lays eggs that hatch into baby bees. Worker bees feed and care for her. A queen may live for up to five years.

A **drone** is a male bee. Drones mate with the queen so that she can lay eggs. Drones die after mating.

There is only one queen in a colony. She lays up to 1500 eggs a day.

The queen is the biggest bee in the colony.

Ready, Set, Grow!

A bee goes through different stages as it grows. Can you count them? Start with the egg.

 **1 Egg**

The queen lays an egg in a cell. The egg is smaller than the dot on this i.

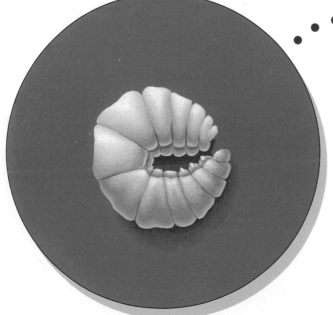

2 Larva

A larva hatches from the egg. Workers feed the larva up to 200 times a day. At first, the larva eats a jelly made by the workers. Later, the larva eats pollen mixed with honey.

3 Pupa

Workers seal the cell with wax. Inside the cell, the larva spins a cocoon. Now, it is a pupa. The pupa grows and changes.

4 Adult

The pupa turns into an adult bee. The bee chews through the wax to get out of the cell. The bee is fully grown and ready to work.

Workers feed a special "royal jelly" to a few baby bees. They turn into queens.

Sweet Treat

Worker bees gather food for the colony. They take pollen and nectar from flowers. They carry this food back to the hive.

Bees dance to tell other bees where to find pollen and nectar. A **round dance** says there are flowers close to the hive.

A **waggle dance** says the flowers are far away. It also tells the bees which way to fly.

Honeybees turn nectar into honey so they can eat it. They store some of the honey in cells and cover it with wax. This honey will be food for winter.

In its lifetime, a bee makes less than a small spoonful of honey.

Sip a Shake

A bee uses its long, thin tongue to sip nectar.
You can make a honey milkshake and use a
straw to sip it. Have an adult help you.

What you need

- 125 mL ($\frac{1}{2}$ c.) vanilla ice cream
  or frozen yogurt
- 125 mL ($\frac{1}{2}$ c.) milk
- 30 mL (2 tbsp.) liquid honey
- 250 mL (1 c.) sliced strawberries,
  peaches or bananas
- a blender
- a straw

What you do

1 Put the first three ingredients
into a blender. (For a thicker
shake, add more ice cream.)

2 Add the fruit to the blender
and blend until smooth.

3 Pour into two glasses. Slip in
a straw and sip like a bee.

Safety note: Do not feed honey
to babies under eighteen months.

What's happening?

To make honey, a bee dries nectar on its tongue. Once the nectar is thick, the bee swallows it. The nectar turns to honey in the bee's honey stomach. The bee brings up the honey from its stomach and stores it in the hive.

23

Bee Buddies

Bees need flowers for food. But flowers need bees, too. They are buddies in nature.

Bees carry pollen from flower to flower. The flowers use the pollen to make seeds. The seeds grow into new plants.

Pollen drops here.

Seeds grow here.

A bee may visit thousands of flowers a day.

Yellow pollen sticks to the bee's body. The pollen came from other flowers the bee visited. Some of the pollen will drop onto this flower. Then new seeds begin to form.

Flower Power

Flowers need bees to carry pollen for them.
Can you design a flower that would attract a bee?
Ask an adult to help you.

What you need
- an egg carton
- scissors
- green pipe cleaners
- a paint brush
- bee-friendly decorations,
  such as poster paint, spray
  perfume, glitter and glue

What you do

1 Cut a cup from an egg
carton.

2 Cut petals to make a landing
place for a bee.

3 Decorate your flower to
make it bee friendly. You
might paint the petals, spray on
a sweet scent or make pollen
with glitter and glue.

4 Push the end of a pipe
cleaner through the flower to
make a stem. Bend the end to
keep it in place.

What's happening?
Bees like flowers with:
- blue, purple or yellow colors
- sweet smells
- tasty pollen and nectar
- a good landing spot

Look outside for real flowers that bees would be attracted to.

Bees and Us

Honeybees are important to us. They make honey and help fruits and vegetables grow.

In the spring, bees carried pollen to the blossoms on this tree. Now the tree is full of apples.

To make a small jar of honey, bees must visit 2 million flowers.

This is a beekeeper, a person who raises bees and gathers honey for us to eat. The beekeeper takes honey from the hive without hurting the bees.

Other Bees

There are more than 25 000 kinds of bees in the world. Here are just a few.

Bumblebee

African cuckoo bee

Sweat bee

Solitary mining bee

Giant mason bee

Bee Words

colony: a group of bees that lives and works together

drone: a male bee that mates with the queen

hive: a home for honeybees

honey: a food made by honeybees from the nectar of flowers

honeycomb: rows of wax cells inside a hive

mate: when the queen and a drone come together to produce eggs

nectar: a sweet flower juice that bees turn into honey

pollen: a flower dust that is used to form seeds

queen: a bee that lays all the eggs in a colony

royal jelly: a rich food that turns a baby bee into a queen

swarming: when a big group of bees, including the queen, flies away from its hive to start a new hive

worker: a female bee that does the day-to-day work of the hive

Index

First published in the United States, Great Britain, Canada, Australia, and New Zealand in
2006 by North-South Books Inc., an imprint of NordSüd Verlag AG, Gossau Zürich, Switzerland.
Distributed in the United States by North-South Books Inc., New York.

Library of Congress Cataloging-in-Publication Data is available.
A CIP catalogue record for this book is available from The British Library.

ISBN-13: 978-0-7358-2087-6 / ISBN-10: 0-7358-2087-2 (trade edition)
10 9 8 7 6 5 4 3 2 1

Printed in Belgium

Snow Leopards

By Nicole Poppenhäger
Illustrated by Ivan Gantschev

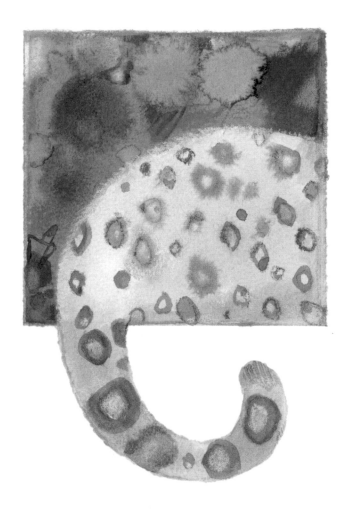

Translated by J. Alison James

NORTHSOUTH BOOKS
New York / London

Simi came into the world just a few minutes after his sister, Siri. Unlike her, Simi was born weak. Drinking Mother's milk strengthened him a little, but after a few sips, he fell asleep. Siri nursed next to him until her belly bulged like a ball. It looked as if only one of the snow leopard cubs would make it.

Simi pulled through, though. He was small, much smaller than his sister, but he drank greedily, and day-by-day he grew stronger.

The two cubs fought like kittens, and stronger Siri usually won, but not always. Simi could roll around and escape from his sister's paws, much to her astonishment. He could tuck himself into the narrowest gap, and lie there in wait. Suddenly he would pounce. And when he'd caught her, he held her down so she couldn't move.

The two of them sharpened their claws on the trunks of gnarled shrubs until the bark hung in shreds.

Their mother taught them the rules of the hunt. Patience was the most important rule, and the most difficult. Only a leopard who could be motionless, silent, and make himself almost invisible could catch his prey. People called snow leopards the Ghosts of the Mountain. Siri and Simi, however, were more like Goblins of the Mountain, scrappy, playful, and careless. And hungry! Mother's milk alone did not satisfy the siblings any longer. They had to get better at their hunting. Together they captured their first mountain sheep.

One day the sky was gray-white and silence lay over the mountain. It grew cold. Flakes fell from the sky so thickly that they could no longer see the nearby rocks. Mother warned them of the dangers of the snow. "It is soft and has no teeth and claws, but it comes from all sides. It can fly faster than an eagle diving for a hare."

Siri and Simi curled up close to their mother deep in a cave. A strong wind whirled, pushing the snow all the way back into the cave. The wind hissed and howled like a giant wounded animal who wanted to catch them. They pulled back as far as they could. Here they were safe.

The next day everything had changed. The rocks were almost completely covered with a thick snow blanket. Carefully, Simi and Siri came out of their cave. Although their paws were wide and thick with fur, they sank again and again up to their bellies into the white. Everything went slower than before. Simi and Siri licked the snow. It was refreshing and cold, but they were hungry, and there was nothing in sight.

Their mother decided to lead them down into the valley where there was a forest. There they would find other animals.

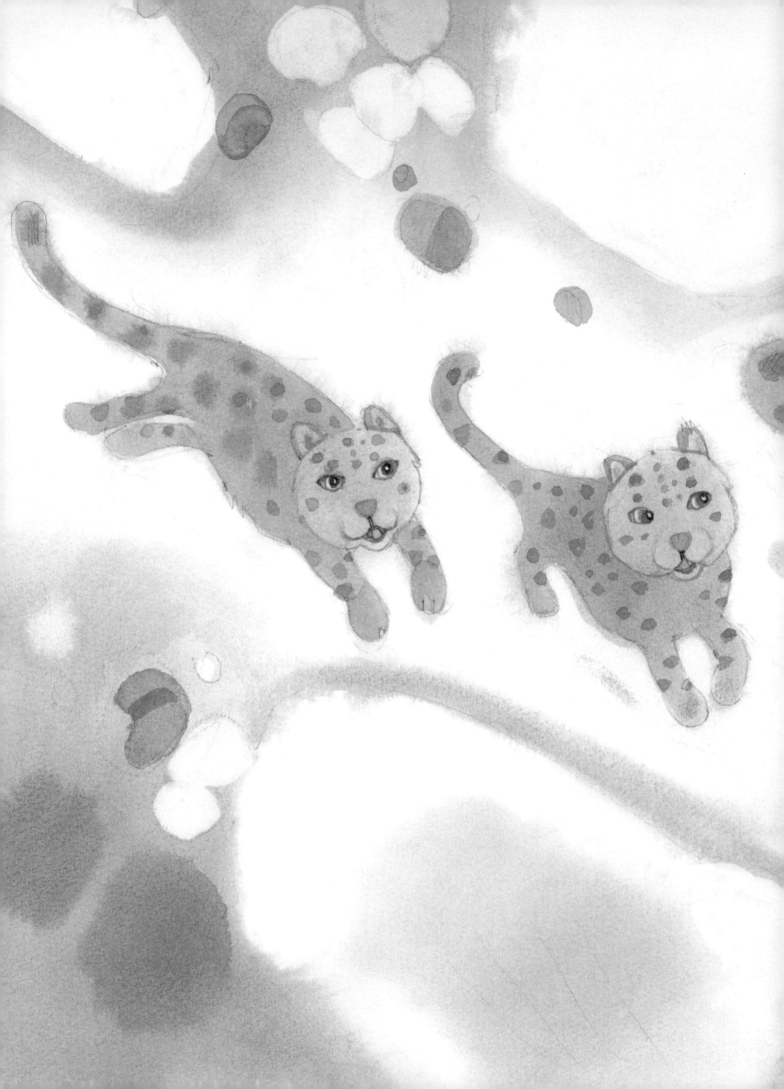

On their way down they had to cross a snowfield. Their mother crossed the slippery surface first, and Siri and Simi followed. All of a sudden, they heard a loud, growling rumble. They knew it was something dangerous!

Mother tensed her body for a spring. She slipped when she rose, skidded on her belly, and sprang again. Simi and Siri followed her. They ran and leaped as fast as they could.

Suddenly the snow was all around them. It took Simi's breath away, it blew into his ears. His sister and mother had disappeared. Simi leaped, but suddenly there was no more ground beneath his paws. The snow was everywhere, under, over, on all sides, even inside him, in his ears, his eyes, his nose, even his mouth was full of the cold, white snow.

He was hurled and thrown around as if someone were playing with him, as he sometimes played with the little snow rabbit. Simi was tossed around faster and faster. Then everything went dark.

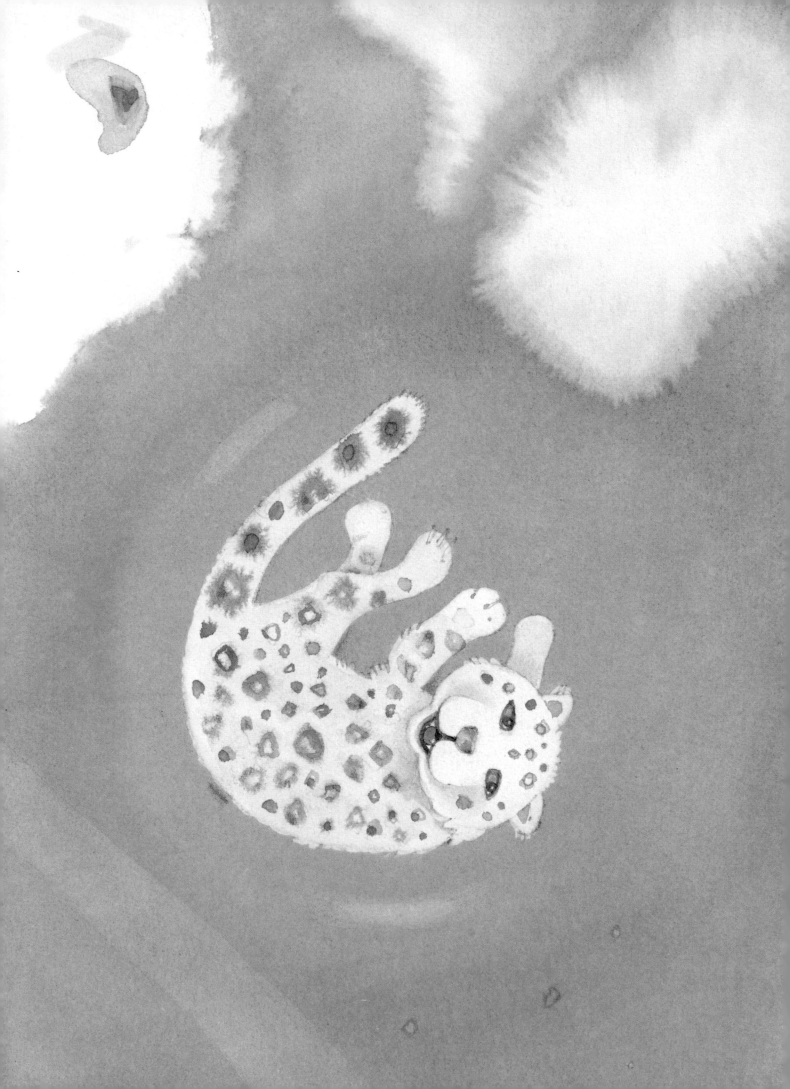

Simi was cold and squashed. It hurt to breathe. Simi tried to stretch his limbs. He didn't want to be trapped. He wanted to breathe. He needed air. Air! Simi scratched and clawed at the snow. He didn't know which way was up and which was down. But he managed to move. He stopped feeling pain. He dragged his body out of the avalanche's snow, into freedom.

With a great shake, he got all the snow from under his fur. He breathed the fresh air and looked out across the sky. He was exhausted. He crawled deep under the branches of a nearby bush and went right to sleep.

When Simi woke, his paws and one of his ears hurt. For the first time in his life, he was all alone. He was so young. How would he find his mother and sister?

The mother snow leopard and Siri had avoided the avalanche and climbed with great care farther down the mountain. It was tiring for both of them, and when they finally reached the first trees of the valley, the mother lay down.

But Siri could find no peace. She wanted to search for her brother.

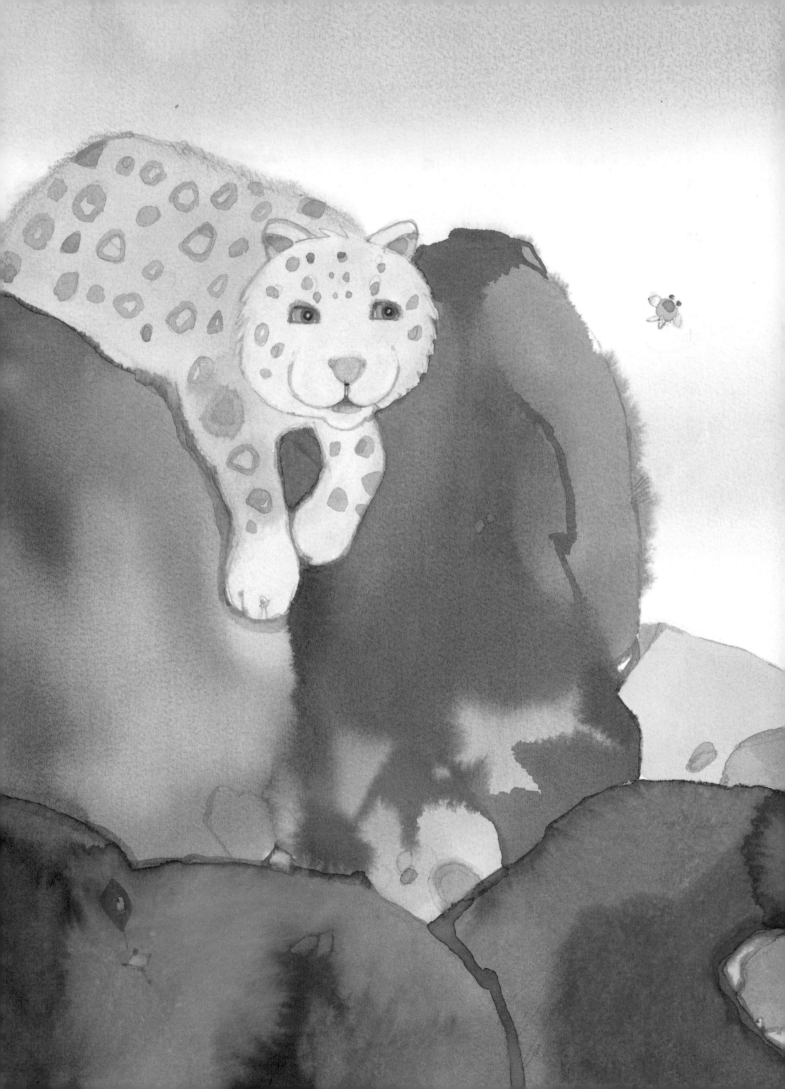

Siri crossed the woods. She sensed that Simi
could not be far. She was sure he was alive. He
had to have escaped the wall of snow that had
come down on them.

She rushed through the woods. She didn't
watch where she was going. Suddenly something
hard snapped over her hind leg. Like teeth, it
held her fast. Siri fell to the ground. Her leg hurt.
But even worse—she could not get loose. She
was trapped. Trembling with fear, Siri lay without
fighting, trying to save her energy.

Siri was lucky. It wasn't hungry wild animals who found her, but men who were in the wilderness to help protect animals.

They approached her in a strange way and made soft calming noises. Siri shivered a little, but she didn't snarl. Her body was tensed and ready to escape.

When the game wardens released the trap, Siri didn't put up a fight. As soon as the iron claws let loose, she darted away as fast as her wounded leg could carry her. Silently, she vanished into the evening darkness.

Siri couldn't run for long. She was in pain and very tired. She saw
a thick bush that looked like a safe lair. She was too exhausted to look
farther. But when she crawled in under the branches, she heard a
threatening growl. Another snow leopard had already taken this place.
It was a young snow leopard, missing a piece of an ear.

But that didn't matter. It was Simi! Siri had found her brother. Happily,
they licked each others' wounds. They lay close together, keeping each
other warm as they slept. In the morning, they would find their way
back to their mother.

Snow Leopards

Snow leopards like Simi and Siri are endangered animals. They are difficult for researchers to study, not only because of their natural camouflage, but also because they are shy and elusive animals. There are estimated to be fewer than 7,000 left in the wild today. Unfortunately, snow leopards have long been hunted for their extremely soft fur and their bones, which are used in traditional Chinese medicines. Humans have taken over more and more of the snow leopards' habitat with farming, leaving less room for the wild animals that snow leopards eat.

Snow leopards are fearsome hunters capable of hunting animals three times their size. They eat a wide range of animals, from small mammals like mice, hares, and marmots, to large animals like wild sheep, deer, goats, ibex, and boar. Snow leopards can require a home range as large as 100 square miles (259 sq km) in places where prey is scarce.

Snow leopards live at high elevations—from 9,800 to 14,800 feet (3,000 to 4,500 m), and even higher in the Himalayas—and can be found in many countries, including Afghanistan, Pakistan, India, China, Tibet, and Russia. They prefer steep, broken terrain like cliffs and ravines to forests, because the rocky surfaces hide their gray coats while giving them an excellent view of their prey.

Because of the cold climates where they live, their thick fur, which is predominantly gray with black-and-brown ring markings, can be as much as five inches long on their bellies. They have short forelimbs and long hind limbs, which give them the agility they need for hunting. Their paws are covered with fur that provides insulation and increases the surface area of the foot, acting almost like a snowshoe. Their thick furry tails are nearly as long as their bodies and serve as balancing tools for the leopards while climbing or jumping. Together, their tails and furry paws give them the ability to jump, spring, and pounce on prey as far as 45 feet (14 m) away.

Solitary by nature, females give birth to one to four cubs in rocky caves lined with the mother's fur. Just like Simi and Siri, young cubs follow their mother on hunts starting at about three months of age and will spend their first winter with her before setting off to find their own ranges.